RAMPAGE OF THE ROBOTS

Sam Watkins
Tom McLaughlin

Pictures by
Bill Ledger

OXFORD
UNIVERSITY PRESS

OXFORD
UNIVERSITY PRESS

Great Clarendon Street, Oxford, OX2 6DP,
United Kingdom

Oxford University Press is a department of the University of Oxford.
It furthers the University's objective of excellence in research, scholarship,
and education by publishing worldwide. Oxford is a registered trade mark of
Oxford University Press in the UK and in certain other countries

© Oxford University Press 2020

The moral rights of the author have been asserted

First published 2018
This edition published 2020

All rights reserved. No part of this publication may be reproduced, stored in a retrieval system, or transmitted, in any form or by any means, without the prior permission in writing of Oxford University Press, or as expressly permitted by law, by licence or under terms agreed with the appropriate reprographics rights organization. Enquiries concerning reproduction outside the scope of the above should be sent to the Rights Department, Oxford University Press, at the address above.

You must not circulate this work in any other form
and you must impose this same condition on any acquirer

British Library Cataloguing in Publication Data
Data available

9780192776082

1 3 5 7 9 10 8 6 4 2

Paper used in the production of this book is a natural, recyclable product made from wood grown in sustainable forests. The manufacturing process conforms to the environmental regulations of the country of origin.

Printed in China

Acknowledgements
Illustrations by Bill Ledger
Activities by Rachel Russ
Design by James W Hunter
Photo assets supplied by shutterstock.com, cgtrader.com, turbosquid.com.

CONTENTS

Helping your child to read................................4

Operation Poach..5
Operation Poach activities........................ 37

The Termite-nator 39
The Termite-nator activities......................... 71

Helping your child to read

Before they start
- Talk about the back cover blurb. Ask your child whether they know what a termite is. Encourage them to say how they think Evan and Nisha might defeat a giant robotic termite.
- Look at the front cover. Ask your child to suggest what they think the dark shadow in the picture might be. Read the title together and talk about the meaning of the word 'rampage'.

During reading
- Let your child read at their own pace – don't worry if it's slow. They could read silently, or read to you out loud.
- Help them to work out words they don't know by saying each sound out loud and then blending them to say the word, e.g. *e-x-p-l-ai-n-ed, explained*.
- Encourage your child to keep checking that they understand what they're reading. Remind them to reread to check the meaning if they're not sure.
- Give them lots of praise for good reading!

After reading
- Look at pages 37 and 71 for some fun activities.

OPERATION POACH

Sam Watkins

Pictures by
Bill Ledger

In this story ...

Jin **(SWOOP)**

Jin has the power to fly. He once had a race with a jumbo jet ... and won! He can fly high enough to reach outer space!

Cam **(SWITCH)**

Cam has the power to turn into different animals. She once stopped some baddies from robbing a bank by turning into a giraffe.

1
HAPPY BIRTHDAY, JIN!

"**AAAAARGH!**"

As Jin entered the common room, he tripped, stumbled and landed in a heap at Cam's feet. A stupendously long scarf was tangled round his legs.

Cam helped Jin up. "That's some scarf!"

"It's a birthday present from Gran, to stop me getting cold on missions," Jin explained. "I think she got a bit carried away knitting it."

Cam laughed and pulled a package out from behind her seat. "Happy birthday!"

Jin tore the paper off. "Deluxe, all-weather flying goggles! Thanks, Cam."

Just then, a big screen on the wall flickered into life and the Head of Hero Academy appeared.

"Ah, Jin and Cam," the Head said. "I need you in my office right away. I have just had Police Commissioner Jordan on the phone."

Jin and Cam looked at each other excitedly. That usually meant a mission.

"**Let's go!**" Jin said.

When they arrived at the Head's office, the Head showed them a picture of a bald man wearing glasses.

"It's that bird guy from TV," said Cam.

The Head nodded. "Professor Poach has gone missing in the Chilly Isles."

Jin looked worried. "The Chilly Isles are really hard islands to get to, aren't they?" he said.

"Yes, and to make things worse, a blizzard has just blown in," said the Head.

The picture changed to a steep and rocky mountain surrounded by whirling snow clouds.

"Mount Stormpeak is the tallest mountain in the Chilly Isles," continued the Head. "Professor Poach was studying rare birds there when the storm struck. He sent a message for help, but the rescue helicopter can't get there while the storm's raging. I need you to fly there and find him."

Jin spun into his superhero costume to become Swoop. He wrapped his scarf several times round his neck. "I'm ready!"

"Just a minute," said Cam. She became Switch and changed into a seagull. "**W-AAAA-RK!**" she squawked.

2
THE CHILLY ISLES

Soon, the two superheroes were soaring over a calm, blue sea. They could see a grey smudge on the horizon ahead.

"That must be the Chilly Isles," shouted Swoop.

Switch cawed in reply.

In the distance, dark clouds were looming. Swoop felt the wind buffet him as the clouds drew closer.

"Storm up ahead," Swoop warned Switch, who was falling behind. He slowed down to let her catch up, but then, without warning, a blast of icy wind swept him up. It HURLED him into thick, whirling cloud.

The storm **ROARED** and **TOSSED** Swoop around like a paper bag. Sleet *swirled* in front of his eyes. He switched on the wipers on his goggles but, even then, he could see nothing other than white snowflakes.

Just as suddenly as it had swallowed him up, the storm spat Swoop out again. He found himself **HURTLING** towards a dark cliff face. He managed to swerve up just in time.

"**Phew!** That was close," Swoop muttered, wrapping his scarf around himself more tightly. "This must be Mount Stormpeak." He looked for Switch, but couldn't see her.

Swoop started to fly up the cliff face, looking for Switch and the missing professor.

A speck above him caught his eye, and Swoop breathed a sigh of relief. "A bird," he thought. "It must be Switch."

The speck got BIGGER ... and BIGGER ...

"That's not a seagull. That's an eagle," Swoop thought. "A **GIANT** eagle!" He began to panic as the bird started to dive. "It's heading straight for me!"

3
THE FIEND-5000

Swoop swerved to avoid the giant bird. Just then, his scarf got caught on a spiky bush that was growing on the cliff face. He managed to yank it free but the gigantic eagle seized him and carried him away.

The bird's grip was painfully tight, but Swoop managed to twist his head and look up. To his surprise, instead of feathers, he saw a control panel.

"FIEND-5000," he read. "It's not a bird. It's a **robot!**"

The robot eagle flew straight towards the cliff face.

"**NOOOOOOO!**" Swoop cried.

At the last minute, a rock slid away to reveal a vast cave.

As they flew inside, Swoop saw that the floor of the cave was covered with HUGE, silver eggs. The eagle dropped Swoop amongst them and flapped off.

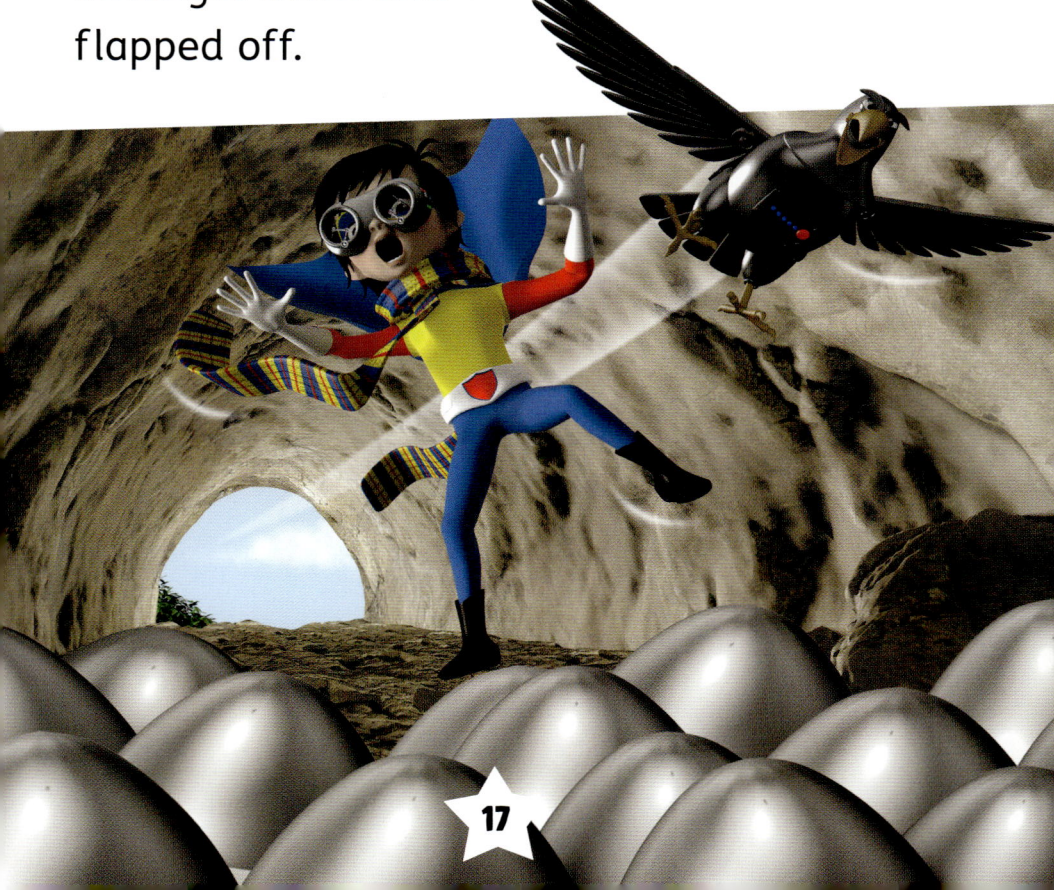

Swoop stared at the egg nearest him. He went to touch it, but a voice made him jump.

"Well, well. A visitor. How **egg-citing**."

Swoop turned to see a bald man wearing glasses walking towards him – the missing professor.

"**Professor Poach!**" Swoop exclaimed. "Are you OK?"

Professor Poach smiled. "How nice of you to ask." Then his smile vanished. "No, I'm **NOT** OK." A wild look came into his eyes. "Those featherbrains in Lexis City didn't give me the Egg-ceptional Birdwatcher of the Year Award – again! I go to the most extreme places to get pictures of the rarest birds. Do I get any recognition? Never."

The professor smiled a nasty smile. "They'll change their tune when I set my army of Feathered Fiends free."

"Feathered ... *fiends*," Swoop repeated, remembering the name on the robot bird that had grabbed him. The **FIEND-5000**!

The professor waved at the silver eggs. "When they are fully charged, they'll take over Lexis City – and then, the world. **Tee-hee-hee-hee!**"

PROFESSOR POACH

NUMBER 11 — MOST WANTED VILLAIN

Catchphrase: How egg-citing!
Hobbies: birdwatching, playing the accordion.
Likes: eggs-periments, eggs-tra strong mints.
Dislikes: feather duvets, quilted jackets, feather dusters. (Feathers belong on birds!)
Beware! Poach will stop at nothing to win the Egg-ceptional Birdwatcher of the Year Award!

4
CAPTURED!

"I must stop those robot birds!" cried Swoop, launching himself into the air. "Aaaarrgh!"

He was yanked back to the ground – his scarf had caught on a bit of metal sticking out of one of the egg cups.

Professor Poach leaned over and quickly tapped on a keypad on the wall next to him.

A large cage fell out of the darkness above – and landed over Swoop.

"This should keep you out of my way," the professor said. "Now, we just have to wait for all your friends to show up so I can trap them, too. The last thing I need is a load of heroes interfering with my plans for world domination."

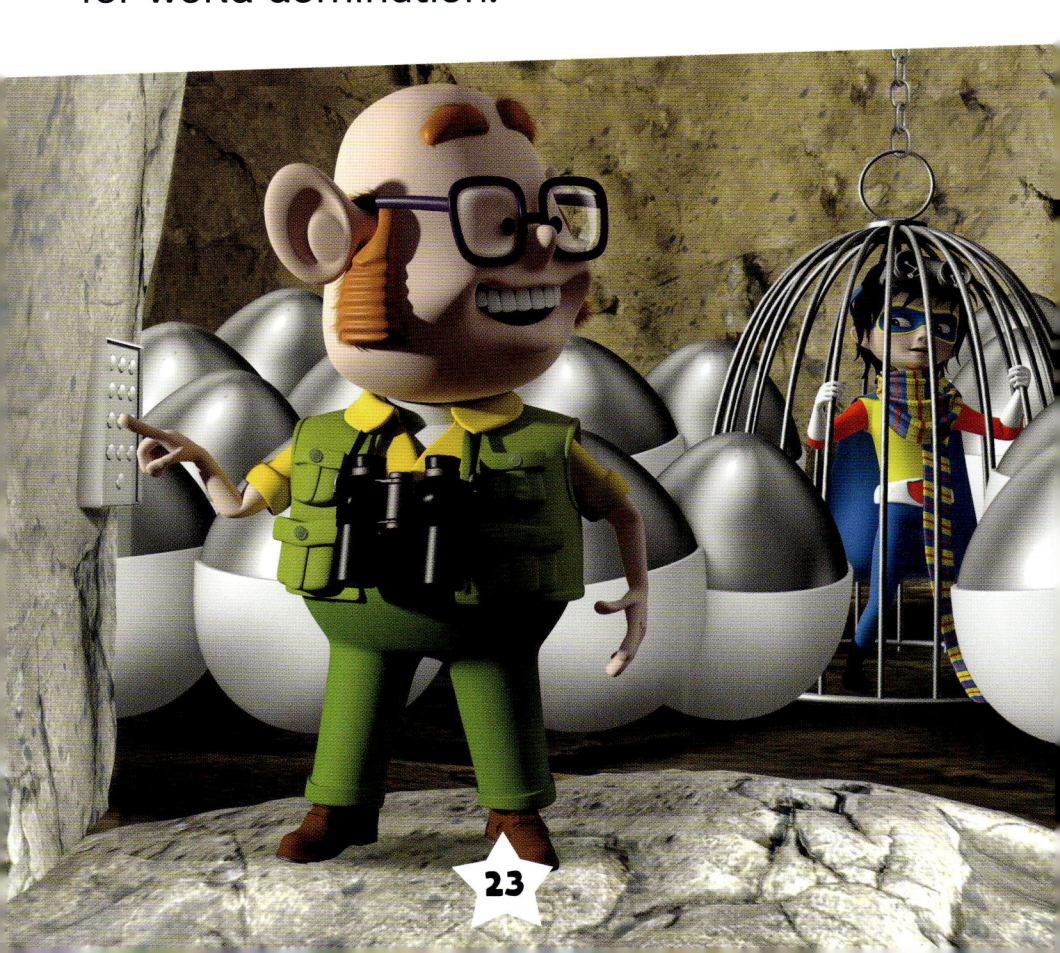

There was a clatter from across the cave. Poach frowned. "What was that?"

He rushed off to investigate.

"You won't get away with this!" Swoop yelled, as Poach disappeared deep into the cave.

Suddenly, Swoop heard a soft caw. A seagull was flying towards him. It landed next to the cage.

"**Switch!**" Swoop exclaimed. "You found me! Quick – help me get out."

Swoop pointed at the keypad on the wall. "You'll need to put in the code."

Switch gave him a confused look.

"Try 1234," Swoop suggested.

Switch pushed the buttons with her beak ... and nothing happened. She tried other combinations. Nothing worked.

"I know," Swoop said, finally. "FIEND-5000! Try 5000, Switch."

She did. The cage flew up, and Swoop was free.

"Let's get out of here!" he cried.

"**Not so fast!**" boomed a voice.

5
SUPER-SCARF POWER

"Professor Poach!" cried Swoop.

As Poach raced towards them, Swoop had a flash of inspiration. He whipped his scarf off and gave one end to Switch. "Here."

Switch grabbed it with her beak. The two superheroes **launched** themselves into the air.

"Super-scarf power!" shouted Swoop. Swoop and Switch flew in circles around the professor, wrapping him up in the scarf until only his head was poking out of the top. Then they flew down.

"Let's put him in the cage," said Swoop. "I want my scarf back."

Switch changed back into a human, and they lowered the cage over Poach. Strangely, the professor was smirking.

"What are you so happy about?" asked Swoop, pulling his scarf free. "You're finished."

"Not quite," grinned Poach.

There was a strange machine-like humming sound.

Swoop looked round. "The eggs!"

C-R-A-A-A-ACK!

Around them, the eggs split open. Inside each egg stood a glassy-eyed robot bird.

"Fiends – activate NOW!" Poach barked.

As Poach spoke, the birds raised their heads. Mechanically, they marched to the cave entrance, where the giant robot eagle was waiting. It took off and flapped out of the cave. All the newly-hatched robot birds followed it.

"**STOP!**" cried Switch, trying to grab one.

Poach laughed. "The only thing that can stop the Feathered Fiends is the FIEND-5000 – oops!"

"FIEND-5000?" Switch said. "What's that?"

Swoop gasped. "It's the giant eagle that caught me. It must be controlling the others." He wrapped his scarf back round his neck. "I'll go after it. You stay with Poach and call Hero Academy. Get them to send a helicopter as soon as they can."

6
EMERGENCY!

Swoop caught up with the Feathered Fiends over the sea, just before they got to Lexis City. He swerved in and out of the flock, overtaking the birds one by one, until he saw the FIEND-5000. It was ahead of the others, and had nearly reached the city.

"How can I stop it?" Swoop wondered.

It was time for super-scarf power again. Swoop unwound his scarf, tied it into a lasso and threw it, catching the eagle's tail. Then Swoop reeled himself in until he was flying just below the robot.

The FIEND-5000 looked down. "**KRA-A-A-AAK!**" it squawked. It started to twist its tail up and down.

Swoop clung desperately to the scarf, as he swung around wildly. Looking up, he noticed a large, red EMERGENCY button on the bird's belly.

"Well, this IS an emergency!" Swoop said to himself. He pressed the button.

"**KRA-A-A-AA-**" The FIEND-5000 froze mid-squawk. Then it dropped down, taking Swoop's scarf with it.

Swoop hurled himself clear, then turned and looked behind him. The rest of the Feathered Fiends were tumbling into the sea.

Later that day ...

Jin walked into the hall at Hero Academy and was hit by a roar of voices.

"**Surprise!**"

He looked around, amazed. There were decorations and balloons, and a huge cake on a table.

"We thought we'd throw you a surprise birthday party," Cam said, grinning.

"My birthday!" exclaimed Jin.

"I almost forgot."

The Head appeared on a screen at the front of the hall. "It's actually a double celebration – your birthday and a successful mission."

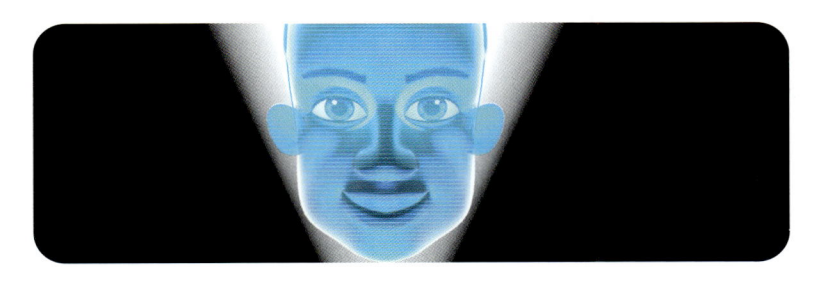

Later on, as Jin was tucking into his third slice of birthday cake, Cam came over carrying a parcel.

"This arrived for you by super-post," she said, handing him the parcel.

Jin ripped it open excitedly. "My scarf!" He held it up, and a note fluttered out. He picked it up.

"Dear Jin, we found your scarf floating in the sea. I thought you might want it back. It helped you crack the case and put that rotten egg, Poach, behind bars. From Police Commissioner Jordan."

Jin laughed. "It really has been an *eggs*-tra special birthday!"

AFTER READING ACTIVITIES

QUICK QUIZ

See how fast you can answer these questions! Look back at the story if you can't remember.

1) What did Jin's gran give him for his birthday?
2) Where on the Chilly Isles do the heroes think Professor Poach has gone missing?
3) What is the name of the giant robot bird that carries Jin into the cave?

THINK ABOUT IT!

Why does Professor Poach want the heroes to come to the Chilly Isles?

SPOT THE DIFFERENCE

Spot the four differences between the pictures of Professor Poach.

Answers: 1) a very long scarf; 2) Mount Stormpeak; 3) FIEND-5000.

THE TERMITE-NATOR

Tom McLaughlin

Pictures by
Bill Ledger

In this story ...

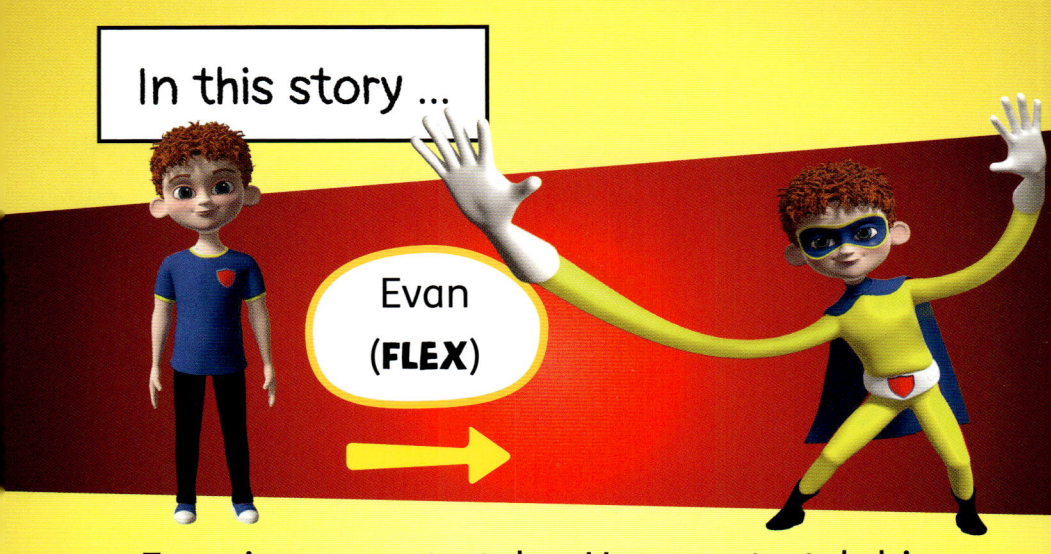

Evan (**FLEX**)

Evan is super stretchy. He can stretch his body in any direction. He once stretched his arms all the way around Hero Academy.

Nisha (**NIMBUS**)

Nisha has the power to control the weather. She can make it sunny or stormy. Once she stopped some baddies by trapping them in a tornado.

1
EVAN'S DILEMMA

Evan was struggling to make a decision. It was the most important decision of his day.
"I just don't know, Nisha. Should I go for raspberry or strawberry?" he asked, scratching his head and staring at the two jars of jam in front of him.

Suddenly, there was a loud rumble. Evan looked up, surprised.

"You'd better decide quickly," Nisha said, through a mouthful of toast. "I can hear your belly growling from here."

"That's not me!" Evan cried out, as the dinner hall wobbled like a jelly. "It's coming from outside!"

Just then, a shrill **BRIIIIING!** filled the air. Alarms all over the school started ringing.

"It's a red alert!" shouted Nisha, clinging on to the table as the room shook again.

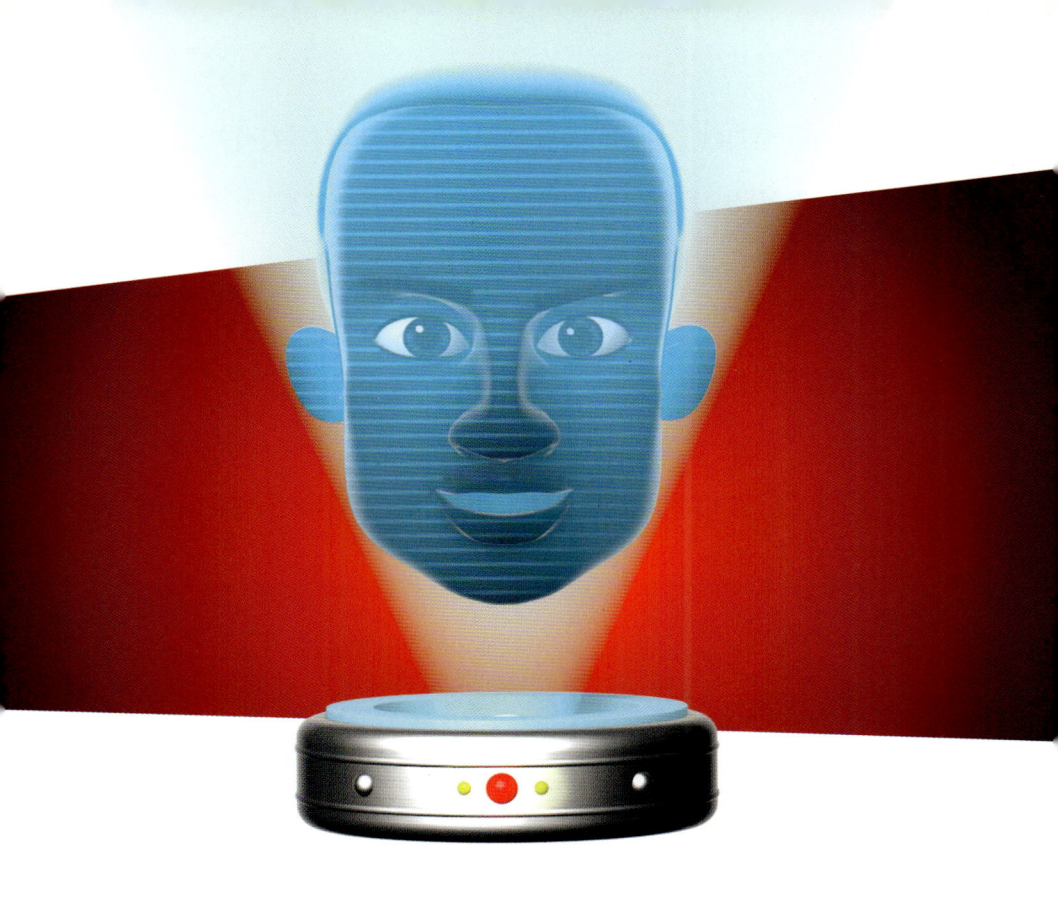

Suddenly, the Head appeared on a screen in the dinner hall. "This is a **BIG** emergency. Lexis City is under attack from a mystery creature!" he said, in alarm. "Nisha, Evan … I need you two to investigate at once. There's no time to lose!"

"We're on our way," Evan said.

"You can count on us," added Nisha.

Nisha and Evan quickly spun into their super suits, becoming Nimbus and Flex. Then they **dashed** to the door.

"**Wait!**" the Head called after them.

"Sir?" Flex said, skidding to a stop.

"If it was up to me," replied the Head with a grin, "I'd go for strawberry every time."

2
ROBOT ALERT!

Nimbus and Flex raced through the streets of Lexis City, following the rumbling noise.

"We're heading towards Police Commissioner Jordan's office!" Flex yelled above the noise, which was getting **louder** and **louder**.

They turned a corner and came to a sudden halt. A **GIGANTIC** robot loomed in front of them.

"It looks like a giant insect!" Flex said, unable to take his eyes off the metal monster.

"**I AM THE TERMITE-NATOR!**" the robot bellowed. Its metallic voice echoed off the buildings. "**OUT OF MY WAY, TINY HUMANS!**" It opened its jaws like a hungry rubbish truck and took a huge bite out of Police Commissioner Jordan's office. Bits of brick and plaster fell out of its giant mouth and landed on the street below.

"I thought *I* was a messy eater!" yelled Flex, diving for cover behind a tree.

Nimbus ducked down next to him. "This is a **disaster!** I hope Commissioner Jordan is all right."

"Uh oh!" Flex exclaimed. "Looks like the Termite-nator is going back for a second helping!"

3
SEE YOU LATER, TERMITE-NATOR

The heroes watched in **horror** as the Termite-nator took another **ENORMOUS** bite out of Police Commissioner Jordan's office. They could see the commissioner inside, glaring at the Termite-nator. She was holding her two terrified dogs, Tick and Tock.

"**How dare you!**" Commissioner Jordan shouted at the gigantic robot. "I will not stand for *anyone* upsetting my dogs."

"We've got to do something!" Flex said to Nimbus.

Just then, the Termite-nator reached out with a huge metal grabber and scooped the commissioner and her dogs into the air. The dogs **yapped** furiously, but the Termite-nator ignored them.

There was a GRINDING noise as the robot's belly opened.

"It's got a cage in there!" Nimbus cried.

The robot put the commissioner and her dogs inside the cage.

"I've got a plan!" Flex said. He held on to the tree that they were hiding behind with one arm. With his other arm, he **stretched** across the street and grabbed on to a lamp-post, so that his arm was stretched like a trip wire.

"Good idea!" exclaimed Nimbus. "I'll get its attention." She ran towards the Termite-nator and waved her arms. **"Hey, you big pile of junk!"** she yelled.

The robotic beast turned towards the heroes.

"Bet you can't catch me," Nimbus shouted, racing back towards the tree and hurdling over Flex's arm.

The Termite-nator stepped effortlessly over Flex. "**HA, HA! YOU CAN'T STOP ME THAT EASILY!**" it bellowed. Then it reached down and yanked up the tree that Flex was wrapped round and threw it on the ground.

Flex snapped back to his normal shape and got away just in time.

"Let me try," Nimbus said to Flex. She summoned up a powerful gust of wind, blowing it towards the Termite-nator. The robot **wobbled**, **stumbled** backwards, then – with an almighty CRASH! – landed in a heap on the ground.

The door to the cage sprang open as the Termite-nator hit the street.

Nimbus and Flex clambered over the rubble to help the commissioner out of the cage.

"Are you OK?" Flex asked the commissioner.

"I'm all right," she replied. "The dogs are a bit shaken up, but they'll be fine ... thanks to you."

Flex breathed a sigh of relief. He smiled at Nimbus. "Job well done!" he said.

Then the Termite-nator began to move again.

4
DOCTOR BUG

"Look! Something's happening to the robot!" Flex said, pointing at the wreckage of the Termite-nator.

Nimbus and the commissioner turned and saw a hatch opening at the top of the Termite-nator's head. Slowly, one hand appeared, then **another** ... and **another!**

A tiny man emerged from the hatch. He was wearing a suit of armour that made him look just like a termite. The antennae on his helmet **wiggled** as he moved. Nimbus and Flex tried not to giggle.

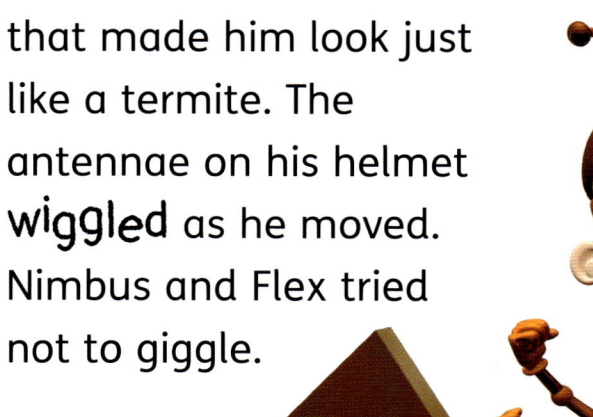

"Nobody move!" shouted the insect man. "Fear the mighty Doctor Bug! I built the Termite-nator to destroy you all! I imagine that I'll be shooting straight to the top of your Most Wanted Villains list, won't I, Commissioner?"

Police Commissioner Jordan snorted with laughter. "**You?** Number one on the Most Wanted Villains list? Hardly."

"And why not?" Doctor Bug demanded.

"Erm ... I think Ray Ranter is number one," Nimbus said.

"**SILENCE!**" shrieked the tiny man.

"Did you do all this just because you wanted to be top of my **Most Wanted Villains** list?" the commissioner asked, raising her eyebrows.

"Yes. I mean, no. I mean ... maybe." He shuffled his feet. "So what number am I on the list? Two?" Doctor Bug asked hopefully.

"More like twenty-two," the commissioner scoffed.

"**WHAT?**" Doctor Bug folded his arms furiously. "I will make it to the top of that list. You'll see."

"Not if you're in jail," said Flex, stretching out an arm to grab him.

The tiny villain dodged out of Flex's way and jumped high in the air. Wings appeared from the back of his insect suit, and he **whizzed** away before Flex could reach him.

DOCTOR BUG

NUMBER 22 MOST WANTED VILLAIN

Catchphrase: Tremble before me, puny humans!

Hobby: going on safari in Wildcroft Woods to spot rare insects.

Likes: pollen squash, honey cake.

Dislikes: magnifying glasses, Venus flytraps.

Beware! This villain may be small but he has armies of robotic insects under his control – so always carry a fly-swatter, just in case!

Actual size (cm)

5
INVASION!

Back at Hero Academy, Evan and Nisha walked into the dinner hall.

"Where is everyone?" Evan said.

"There's a school trip to the lunchbox museum, remember?" Nisha replied.

Evan shrugged. "I'm starving."

He asked nicely, and Mrs Butterworth gave him some more toast.

"I can't believe Doctor Bug got away," muttered Evan, as he dolloped strawberry jam on top.

"At least we saved the commissioner, her dogs, and the city," replied Nisha.

Evan was just about to take a bite of his toast when there was a loud **munching** sound.

"Hey, you did that without even moving your lips!" Nisha said with a laugh.

"That wasn't me," Evan replied, looking around. "It's coming from that wall."

"**WAIT!** There's something outside," Nisha said, rushing to the window. "Look!"

Outside, hundreds of robot termites had surrounded the academy.

"It's a robotic army!" Evan yelled. "They're eating the walls!"

The whole building was being gobbled up by the tiny robots. Doctor Bug was hovering above them, gripping a remote control that he was using to direct the attack.

"I told you I'd be the number one villain!" he yelled into a tiny megaphone. "There's nothing more villainous than getting my termites to eat Hero Academy. **MWAH-HA-HA-HA!**"

Nisha and Evan looked at each other. This pesky villain was turning out to be rather annoying.

The Head appeared on a screen in the dinner hall, but the image kept breaking up. "I seem to have systems in my bugs … I mean bugs in my system!" he cried, before the image disappeared completely.

6
IN A JAM

"We have to do something, or there'll be nothing left of the academy!" Evan said.

"I've got an idea," Nisha replied.

Once again, the two heroes spun into their super suits and raced outside.

Nimbus summoned up a gust of wind to try to blow the termites away, but there were too many of them.

"I'll go after Doctor Bug!" said Flex. He **stretched** his arms and tried to grab the tiny villain, but every time he got close, Doctor Bug just flew even higher out of reach. Before Flex knew what was happening, his arms were **twisted** into a knot.

"I'm stuck," Flex called out. "Completely stuck. Wait ... that's it – **stuck!** I've just had another idea, Nimbus."

"What do you mean?" asked Nimbus, desperately swatting away as many termites as she could.

"Nimbus, can you untangle my arms?" yelled Flex. "I need to get my toast."

"Now is not the time for snacking!" Nimbus shouted back.

"Trust me!" Flex said with a smile.

Nimbus summoned up another gust of wind to carry her into the air. Then she untangled Flex's arms.

"Thanks," said Flex, **stretching** his arm through the open window and grabbing the plate of toast and jam from the dinner hall.

Flex took a particularly jammy piece of toast and hurled it at Doctor Bug. The toast hit the villain and knocked him to the ground.

"Argh! I'm stuck!" Doctor Bug cried, trying to free himself from the jam. "**Bleurgh**. I hate strawberry jam!"

The more Doctor Bug **wriggled** and **struggled**, the more stuck he became. "Help me, robot termites!" he commanded.

His robot army didn't pay him any attention. Doctor Bug furiously jabbed the button on his controller, but nothing seemed to be happening.

"My controller won't work!" Doctor Bug wailed.

"Oh dear," Flex replied. "Is it **jammed?**"

Suddenly, the robot termites stopped in their tracks. They turned and began to scuttle away.

"**Come back!**" Doctor Bug commanded. "You must obey me. I'm the **Number One Villain!**"

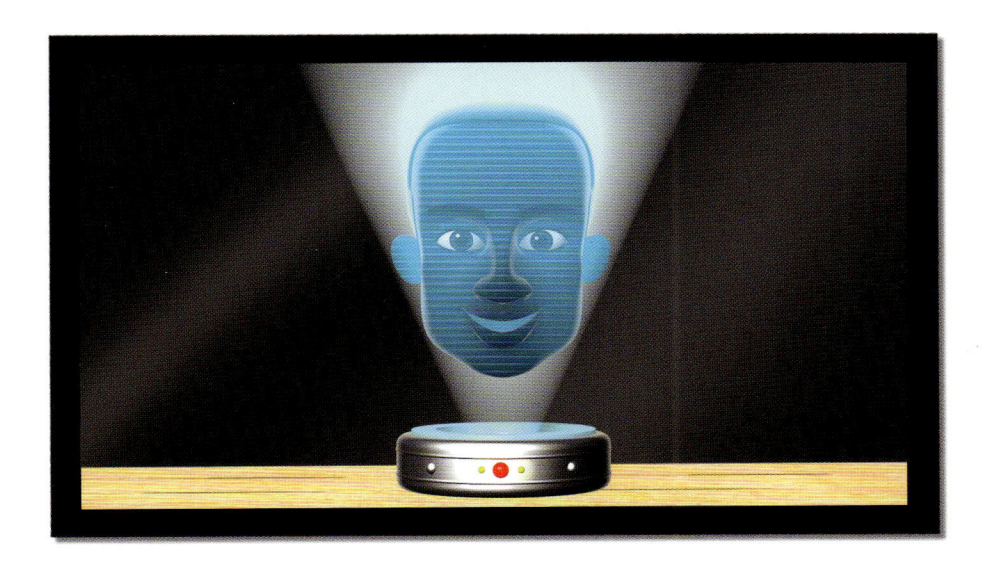

Soon enough, the whole of the robot army was scurrying away.

"**Phew!** We did it," Nimbus said. "What now?"

"Let's go and check on the Head," Flex said. He looked over at the tiny villain. "Doctor Bug isn't going anywhere!"

Inside, the Head appeared on the screen again. "Thank goodness. I'm much better now the bugs have gone," he said. "You two have saved the day … again! Now let's make sure that Doctor Bug is locked away."

The next day, in Lexis City Jail …

"This picture is tiny. You can't even see my face!" Doctor Bug grumbled.

"Breakfast time!" a guard called out, opening the door.

"At least that's something to look forward to," Doctor Bug said. "What's on the menu?"

"Toast." The guard grinned. "I hope you like strawberry jam!"

AFTER READING ACTIVITIES

QUICK QUIZ

See how fast you can answer these questions! Look back at the story if you can't remember.

1) Who goes to investigate the attack on Lexis City?
2) Who climbs out of the hatch opening at the top of the Termite-nator's head?
3) What does Flex use to trap Doctor Bug?

THINK ABOUT IT!

Why might Flex and Nimbus be surprised when Doctor Bug climbs out of the Termite-nator?

TERMITE MAZE

Can you help Evan to get to the jam without meeting any termites?

Answers: 1) Evan and Nisha; 2) Doctor Bug; 3) toast and jam.